LONDON MIDLAND
STEAM ON SHED
LNER STEAM
INDUSTRIAL STEAM
SOUTHERN
STEAM IN ACTION
ARTICULATED LOCOMOTIVES OF THE WOR
SUPERPOWER
AROUND THE WORLD
SCOTTISH
BORDERS STEAM
LIGHT RAILWAYS
standard gauge and narrow gauge
OF BRITAIN
MAIN LINE STEAM
STEAM IN india
SCOTTISH RAILWAYS
in the heyday of steam
GREAT WESTERN
STEAM THROUGH THE YEARS
MIDLANDS
ON THE
WELSH
NARROW GAUGE
WESTERNS
STEAM
SUPERPOWER
BRITISH TRAMS
SCOTTISH
BRANCH LINE
STEAM
THE MIDLAND RAILWAY
the later years of
AROUND THE WORLD
LMSR LOCOMOTIVES
GREAT WESTERN

SOUTHERN STEAM MISCELLANY

in the Southern Steam series

Southern Steam Locomotive Survey: Maunsell Early Classes
Southern Steam Locomotive Survey: Maunsell Later Classes
Southern Steam Locomotive Survey: Bulleid Merchant Navy Pacifics
Southern Steam Locomotive Survey: Bulleid Light Pacifics
Southern Steam Locomotive Survey: Urie Classes
Southern Steam Locomotive Survey: Drummond Classes
Southern Steam Locomotive Survey: Adams Classes
Southern Steam Locomotive Survey: Wainwright Classes
Southern Steam in Action: 1
Southern Steam in Action: 2
Southern Steam in Action: 3
Southern Steam in Action: 4
Southern Steam on Shed
More Southern Steam on Shed
Southern Steam from Lineside
Southern Steam—South and East
More Southern Steam—South and East
Southern Steam—South and West
More Southern Steam—South and West
Southern Steam on the Isle of Wight
Steam on the Brighton Line
Southern Steam in the West Country
More Southern Steam in the West Country
Southern Electrics
Southern Steam in Close-up
Southern Steam—Doubleheaded
Southern Branch Line Steam: 1
Southern Branch Line Steam: 2
Southern Branch Line Steam: 3
Southern Steam 1923-39
Recollections of the Southern between the Wars
Southern Steam through the Years
Southern Steam in Works
Bodmin and Wadebridge Railway

SOUTHERN
STEAM MISCELLANY

TONY FAIRCLOUGH AND ALAN WILLS

D. BRADFORD BARTON LIMITED

2/35LB *ISBN 0 85153 384 1*

printed in Great Britain by H. E. Warne Ltd, London and St. Austell for the publishers

D. BRADFORD BARTON LTD · Trethellan House · Truro · Cornwall

contents

BY PULLMAN TO THE CONTINENT 1929-1972

On 15 May 1929 the Southern Railway introduced the all-Pullman 'Golden Arrow' service between Victoria and Dover which connected with the French 'Fleche d'Or' by way of the SS *Canterbury,* which made the voyage between Dover and Calais in 1hr. 15mins. The overall time for the Victoria-Gare du Nord journey was 6hrs. 35mins. and offered the first class travellers considerable luxury. 'King Arthur' 4-6-0 No.E767 *Sir Valence* is seen near Dover (Marine) shortly after the introduction of the new service in 1929. [D. J. Cobbe Collection]

For a short while after their introduction in 1926 the Maunsell 'Lord Nelsons' were claimed to be Britain's most powerful passenger engines and as such they were soon rostered to the heaviest Continental boat trains. Handled competently by the experienced Stewarts Lane crews, the engines put up some fine performances on these difficult turns. No.858 *Lord Duncan* is seen heading the up 'Golden Arrow' near Shorncliffe on 8 June 1937, the inward service having been diverted to the Boulogne-Folkestone route in 1935. Also, owing to reduced patronage, the Pullman complement of the train had been reduced to four vehicles. [Rev. Arthur C. Cawston]

Pullmans were often employed on special boat trains by the Southern Railway. No.854 *Howard of Effingham* has charge of an up P and O special, seen near Paddock Wood on 6 June 1937. (This photo is of particular interest in that it shows a 'Nelson' in a rarely-seen stage of transformation, ie, the original draughting and chimney arrangements but with modified self-trimming tender). [Rev. Arthur C. Cawston]

A Royal Pullman special, seen east of the tunnels near Sandling on 16 November 1937, has 'LI' 4-4-0 No.1756 as motive power. The train is carrying Leopold, King of the Belgians, on a state visit. [Rev. Arthur C. Cawston]

85

SOUTHERN
1756

E
1
Nº 85

'Lord Nelson' No.859 *Lord Hood* (the unique member of the class rebuilt with 6′ 3″ coupled wheels) accelerates a heavy boat train through Shorncliffe in November 1934. The two Pullmans were provided for Princess Marina, who was en route to London for her wedding to the Duke of Kent.
[Rev. Arthur C. Cawston]

GOLDEN
ARROW
21C1

Channel Packet soon returned to her native haunts at Exmouth Junction shed in the West of England and thereafter the train was usually worked by the smaller 'West Country'/'Battle of Britain' light Pacifics, though the big 'Merchant Navies' appeared at intervals. No.21C119 had gone new to Exmouth Junction but was transferred to the Eastern Section to work from Stewarts Lane in 1947. When seen near Sandling in April 1947 she had not yet been named *Bideford*. [D. T. Cobbe Collection]

Continental traffic ceased abruptly with the outbreak of the Second World War in September 1939 and it was not until 15 April 1946 that the 'Golden Arrow' resumed its service. For the inaugural runs the engine was appropriately No.21C1 *Channel Packet*, the doyen of the 'Merchant Navy' Class. These powerful Pacifics were originally conceived as motive power for the Continental boat trains but had spent the War years hard at work on the Western Section. The suitably decorated engine was still working the Stewarts Lane duty on 22 April 1946 when seen at Bargrove, near Shorncliffe, with the down train. [Rev. Arthur C. Cawston]

The Southern Railway's post-War image: an immaculate brightly-painted locomotive, No.21C140, heads a sparkling Pullman train near Bargrove towards the Continent, 12 April 1947. Of course, this was the view that the Company wished to project and only its prestige trains were in such fine condition in those difficult years of rebuilding. The train formation on view was the standard complement for those early years, consisting of five first class and three second class Pullmans, the *Trianon Bar* car and luggage van.
[Rev. Arthur C. Cawston]

GOLDEN
ARROW
21C140
SOUTHERN
21C140

British Railways continued the Pullman services to the Continent, using Dover (Marine) for the 'Golden Arrow's' connection with SS *Canterbury.* No.34104 *Bere Alston* was only five months old when seen entering Marine station with the down 'Arrow' on 8 September 1950, and the B R Brunswick green paintwork has been well-maintained by the Stewarts Lane cleaner boys. [Rev. Arthur C. Cawston]

Sister Pacific No.34103 *Calstock,* with her injector blowing, eases around the curves at Bargrove on 8 July 1950 with the down Pullman train. Again, the engine is in splendid condition, but it was unfortunate that the shed staff had provided filthy headcode discs for such an important duty. (On other Regions, the two discs above the buffers indicated an express train, but on the Southern these were route indicators for Dover boat trains). [Rev. Arthur C. Cawston]

At times the 'Golden Arrow' service operated via Folkestone Harbour, in which case the trains had to negotiate the difficult three-quarter mile branch which ascended from the harbour to Folkestone Junction on a 1 in 30 incline. The main line locomotives were banned from this line and for many years the rebuilt Stirling 'RI' 0-6-0 tanks were used, often four at a time, in hauling the heavy trains up the bank. One of these stalwarts, No.31337, is about to make a cautious descent from the junction in 1954. [Rev. Arthur C. Cawston]

The 'Golden Arrow' was an important international 'shop window' for British Railways in the early 1950s and the B R hierarchy felt that it would be a suitable duty for their newly-built Standard 'Britannia' Pacifics, and so a pair were allocated to Stewarts Lane shed. One of these, No.70004 *William Shakespeare,* had been exhibited at the Festival of Britain on the South Bank site in 1951 and for this event had been given a special exhibition finish which was retained in pristine condition by 'The Lane'. The engine is seen above at Bargrove in October 1951, shortly after taking up the duty. Below: the second 'Britannia' was No.70014 *Iron Duke.* Unfortunately, on 10 March 1952, she was steaming badly and, having lost 45 minutes getting to Tonbridge the driver stopped for assistance, which was provided in the form of the station pilot, 'Schools' 4-4-0 No.30903 *Charterhouse*, manned by Driver F. George and Passed Fireman G. Whitmore. Luckily a first-class photographer was at hand near Shorncliffe to record the passing ensemble. [Rev. Arthur C. Cawston]

GOLDEN
ARROW
4

30903
30903

The fireman of No.34086 *219 Squadron* fixes the headcode disc in place after the engine had dropped back into Victoria from Stewarts Lane shed. The number five on the disc is the locomotive duty roster number, each depot numbering its duties in a series allocated for the purpose, Stewarts Lane's running from 1 to 80 and 501 to 529. Below: a pair of enormous arrows were fixed to each side of the boiler casings on the Pacifics. The 'Battle of Britain' series of Pacifics were identical to the 'West Countries' but had names very appropriate to the Kentish connection. [C. E. Dann]

Entente Cordiale: the British and French flags were usually flown above the buffer beam of the 'Arrow's' engine. Below: the 'Golden Arrow's' assembly point next to the *Trianon Bar* halfway down the train. A set of new and refurbished Pullmans was allocated to the train during the Festival of Britain in 1951, thus maintaining the luxury travel originally envisaged by the Company's American founder, George M. Pullman, as long ago as 1859, when he converted his initial railway coach to a sleeper. Pullmans first appeared in Britain on the Midland Railway in 1874, and the following year began operating in the South on L B S C R metals. The British Transport Commission made a successful offer for the Company's shares in 1954 and continued to operate most of the services as before.

[C. E. Dann]

The 'Golden Arrow' was worked by men of Number One link at Stewarts Lane shed. These crews rightly enjoyed a high reputation for fine enginemanship on the Southern, as they handled many of the heaviest boat and commuter trains between Victoria and the Coast. Some of their turns were 'rounders' — out via Tonbridge and back through Chatham or vice versa. In spite of intense labour shortages in the post-War years, Stewarts Lane maintained its express engines in good condition, while the state of the 'Arrow' engines became legendary. No.34086 looks superb as her crew enjoy the May sunshine of 1961 (above) or discuss the train tonnage with the guard (below) whilst awaiting departure time at Victoria. [C. E. Dann]

Several of the successful rebuilt 'West Countries' appeared on the 'Golden Arrow' during its final years of steam operation. Although lacking the 'air-smoothed' glamour of the original Bulleids, these engines possessed functional good looks which seemed quite in keeping with the mid-century image. Rebuilt No.34088 *213 Squadron* is seen in action at the site of the proposed new Folkestone (Central) station early in 1961. Note that the rebuilt engine has acquired a pair of suitably smaller arrows which fit the smoke deflectors in lieu of the sidesheets of the original Pacifics. [Rev. Arthur C. Cawston]

Pullmans were often used to carry visiting Royalty and Heads of State who in earlier years arrived on our shores by sea and travelled up to the capital on Southern metals. Although carrying discs denoting a royal train, 'Merchant Navy' 4-6-2 No.35019 *French Line CGT* is hauling a special, conveying Vincent Auriol, President of France, to London on 7 March 1950. The superbly turned-out locomotive, painted in the current B R blue livery of the period, is seen passing Shorncliffe, having been seconded from her normal Nine Elms duties for the special occasion.

[Rev. Arthur C. Cawston]

Royal headcode at Wandsworth Road, this time in honour of the King of Thailand, who was arriving for a state visit on 19 July 1960. No.34088 *213 Squadron* had emerged from Eastleigh Works in rebuilt form only three months previously and was at the time one of 'The Lane's' best locomotives, hence her appearance on this lightweight but prestigious duty. The rebuilt Pacifics were popular with the Eastern Section men, but steam was soon to be but a memory in Kent, as the main phase of the electrification scheme came into operation in June 1961, after which the older locomotives were scrapped while the more modern units such as this Bulleid were transferred to the Western Section for a few more years' service. [L. W. Rowe]

The Pullman boat trains brought glamour to the railway lines of the South East, although particularly at the London end their surroundings were often far from glamorous. Here, rebuilt 'Merchant Navy' No.35025 *Brocklebank Line* propels the mixed stock of the 'Golden Arrow' out of the sidings at Stewarts Lane towards Victoria in readiness for the journey down to Dover in May 1959. The traditional departure was at 11.00 a.m., although the immediate post-War service left an hour earlier, while for some years during the 1950s, including 1959, an unpopular 2.00 p.m. departure was instituted. The last steam-hauled run, behind No.34100 *Appledore,* took place on 11 June 1961, although the S N C F continued to employ Chapelon Pacifics for part of the 'Fleche d'Or's' journey until January 1969. In England the train remained as a luxury electrically-hauled service until October 1972, when the e.m.u. finally conquered. The photographs on the previous pages serve as a reminder of those great trains of yesteryear which in their day were the epitome of gracious living.

[Peter Winding]

PORTRAIT OF THE 'Q1's

The locomotive world of 1942 was staggered by the appearance of Bulleid's 'Q1' 0-6-0s, for surely even the acute shortages of wartime could not justify such an austere and ugly design of engine. Yet truth to tell, the need for the conservation of scarce and valuable metals came second to another overriding consideration. That was the need to design a machine which could travel over the majority of the Southern's routes, yet was powerful enough to handle the heaviest freights which war conditions demanded. Bulleid's solution was this 0-6-0, the like of which had not been seen before (or since). No.C22 is undergoing a minor overhaul in Eastleigh Works on 20 September 1947. [H. C. Casserley]

Construction of the forty 'Q1s' was shared between Ashford (Nos.C17-36) and Brighton (Nos.C1-16/37-40) and all were completed in 1942 at a cost of just under £10,000 apiece. They were soon hard at work on freight trains on the Western Section; No.C20 is seen at Eastleigh, one of ten which went new to that important depot.
[K. J. Marden]

Bulleid could have built more of his predecessor's orthodox 'Q' Class 0-6-0s, but these engines were not without their problems, the most significant being that of poor steaming ability, so he took the basic design of frames and by using similarly-sized cylinders and wheels his locomotive could be classed as a development of the earlier Maunsells. Bulleid emphasised the need for the biggest possible boiler to be used with a large firebox to match. By utilising the 'Lord Nelson' pressings for the Belpaire firebox, a fine steam producer was evolved which had a significant increase of heating surface over that of the 'Q' (1,690 sq. ft. compared with 1,432 sq. ft.). [A. R. Butcher]

Special care was taken in the design of the front end of these engines so that they could be used if required on passenger trains. It was found that they were quite comfortable up to 70 m.p.h. or thereabouts, although the Civil Engineer did not look too favourably on such speeds by engines not having the benefit of any carrying wheels at the front. This lightweight three-coach Tonbridge to Sevenoaks local, seen at Hildenborough in July 1959 with Nos.33037 and 33009 at the head, has their combined tractive effort of 60,000lbs available as power! [Derek Cross]

Bulleid-Firth-Brown double-disc wheels were fitted to the 'Q1's, these helping to keep down the overall weight of the engine. This came to 51½ tons, all of which was available for adhesion, which, with 30,000lbs. of tractive effort, made these machines strong pullers. Above No.33017's number may be seen the B R power classification of 5F followed by the Southern's A, which implied top-rated freight status. Indeed, the main preoccupation of 'Q1' drivers was stopping rather than starting heavy freight trains as their braking power did not match their full hauling capacity. If a 'head' of vacuum-braked vehicles was not available it was not uncommon to make use of two brake vans. No.33017 faces Drummond 'M7' No.30133 across the turntable at the rear of Three Bridges shed, October 1963. [A. R. Butcher]

The fireman is busy charging his firebox while the driver of No.33023 awaits the 'right-away' from Wimborne with a Poole to Eastleigh goods in November 1960. The footplate controls were carefully sited on all Bulleid's engines, these 0-6-0s having a lift-up regulator handle instead of the pull-out type fitted to the Pacifics, with a steam reverser (to save weight); the fireman's injector controls were fitted on the righthand side of the cab. [G. A. Richardson]

No.33003, recently ex-works after a general overhaul, at the coal stage at Ashford shed, 18 March 1961. After twenty years of service their strange outline had become quite acceptable to the discerning onlooker while to the professional railwayman 'handsome is as handsome does', and the 'Q1's were a most useful part of any shedmaster's allocation of locomotives. These engines had a large grate area for their size, 27 sq. ft., and could burn a considerable quantity of fuel when working heavy trains, but the consumption was not excessive in view of the work they could perform. Above the boiler on the coal stage may be seen the wheeled 'tubs' which will be used to top up the tender's five tons capacity. [D. T. Cobbe]

No.33006 of Feltham, seen on shed at Hither Green, with a mixed traffic companion of a previous generation. The design of the 'N' Class Moguls dates back to 1917, No.31852, seen here on 11 March 1961, having been built in 1925 at Ashford from parts manufactured in Woolwich Arsenal. Neither class of engine depicted here could be regarded as a glamorous type, yet over the years they performed their arduous duties with reliability and helped to keep freight and secondary passenger services on the move. The 'N's were a familiar sight from East Kent to North Cornwall; the 'Q1's rarely penetrated west of Salisbury, but were seen almost everywhere else on the Southern. [D. T. Cobbe]

In order to keep down the total weight, everthing which was considered non-essential was omitted from the 'Q1' design, among which were the traditional running boards and splashers. At first the footplatemen were unnerved at the sight of the whirling coupling rods, particularly when speeding with a passenger train, but as Bulleid himself pointed out, the thin metal of a running board would provide scant protection should one of the rods break. Here, No.33039 is seen at the closed station of Amesbury on the Bulford branch on 10 March 1963.
[A. R. Butcher]

The excellent boilers were manufactured at Eastleigh and were of traditional type, tapering from 5′ 9″ to 5′ 0″, but were lagged with Idaglass which, while providing insulation, could not support a normal boiler cladding, hence the adoption of the curved casing which gave the engines an 'air-smoothed' contour. Small covers were provided to allow access to the boiler fittings, though these covers were often left opened or even removed altogether, as has been the clack valve cover of No.33039 (Amesbury, 10 August 1963). The live steam injectors are paired beneath the fireman's side of the cab, access to which is provided by means of a single ladder fixed at the front end of the tender. [A. R. Butcher]

035
TRAINS
CROSS
HERE

The unique profile of the smokebox was dictated by the arrangement of the superheater header and the main steam pipes which led directly to the cylinder block beneath. The flat bottom of the smokebox permitted a tight joint with the cylinder block. As a further aid to lightness the smokebox door was held closed by clips instead of the more usual central dart. Although primarily a freight design the engine carried steam heat connection hoses at front and rear. No.33027 is seen at Tunbridge Wells (West) on 22 March 1964. [A. R. Butcher]

No.33035 runs around her train at Bentley after traversing the Bordon branch. The tenders, carrying five tons of coal and 3,700 gallons of water, were constructed with weight savings in mind. Much use was made of welding techniques and the thinnest possible steel sheeting was used. As a result these vehicles did not stand up to the rough usage of freight working and had to be strengthened in the post-War years. This tender shows signs of patching and repairing. The fire irons were carried in a trough on the left-hand side of the tender top, which also served as a lookout when running tender first. The steel ladders for access to the rear water filler are of typical Bulleid design. [A. R. Butcher]

Lashed by heavy rain, No.33035 returns, tender first, up the branch from Bordon to Bentley with a special on 14 March 1964. The tenders were designed for comfortable rearward running, having a canvas canopy across the top connecting the tender cab to the locomotive. It will be noticed that some nostalgic person has carefully cleaned the locomotive's number so that it resembles its original identity, No.C35. [A. R. Butcher]

LCGB
THE WEALDSMAN
RAIL TOUR
33027
LCGB
33027

A pair of 'Q1's, Nos.33027 and 33006, pull away from Baynards in the evening sunshine with a farewell tour of the Horsham-Guildford line before its complete closure, 13 June 1965. The mechanical lubricator, working off the lefthand front wheel, may be seen clearly; these lubricators were fitted to most of the class after the original displacement lubricators had not proved entirely satisfactory. The sandboxes for the steam sanding gear are placed in front of each pair of wheels. These were extremely easy to fill, in contrast to those on the Pacifics. The leading engine has suffered a scorched smokebox door and has been given a quick patch of black paint.
[A. R. Butcher]

The 'Q1's worked transfer freights to other Regions in the London area and penetrated to Didcot on Western Region with freight traffic. However, this enthusiasts' special took No.33006, along with 'U' Class 2-6-0 No.31639, to Stratford-on-Avon on 7 March 1965. All Maunsell's locomotives were carefully styled, resulting in neat workmanlike engines, while the Bulleid seems to display naked power. [A. R. Butcher]

No.33020 shunts the stock of a special to the west of Chichester before running down the old Midhurst branch to Lavant, 3 October 1965. It will be noticed how the profile of the cab and tender matches that of the Bulleid carriages of the train. [A. R. Butcher]

The first member of the class to be withdrawn, No.33028, succumbed in February 1963, the last active member, No.33006, remaining in operation until April 1966. Final mileages were around the half-million mark, the survivors working out of Guildford shed, which was also the first depot to receive a permanent allocation. Fortunately it was decided to preserve the pioneer engine, which is seen at Brighton on 6 July 1974 in the company of two other classic Southern engines, 'M7' 0-4-4T No.245 and Beattie '0298' 2-4-0WT No.30587. It is interesting to note that almost thirty years after the Second World War ended, the sliding blackout shutters are still in place on the front of the tender. [D. T. Cobbe]

2
33020
33020
LCGB

33001
245
L S W R

The steam chests and 19″ × 26″ cylinders of the 'Q1' show up well in this view of No.33001 undergoing restoration to full working order at Sheffield Park on the Bluebell Railway, 29 August 1977. It is indeed fortunate that the final design of that most typical British type, the 0-6-0 goods engine, has one example retained for posterity. Many thousands were built throughout the long years of steam working. This final example was a worthy member of the class and certainly contained many unique features, not the least being its splendid boiler pressed to the high figure of 230lbs. per sq. in. It is greatly to be hoped that she will soon be in running order so that the present generation may look with awe on her whirling side rods and listen to the sharp rasping exhaust as in the days of yore. [Brian Morrison]

ALONG THE NORTH DEVON LINE

After many years of devious planning by various concerns, broad gauge trains commenced running between Exeter and Barnstaple on 1 August 1854. In 1862 the L S W R took over the lease of the North Devon Railway and the gauge became mixed, with the broad gauge disappearing entirely by 1892. This line diverged from the L S W R's Plymouth route at Coleford Junction, three-quarters of a mile from Yeoford and thirteen miles west of Exeter (Central). Ivatt Class '2' 2-6-2T No.41322 pauses briefly at Coleford Junction box on 28 March 1963 in order to set down water containers for use by the signalmen. [W. L. Underhay]

34017
DEVON
BELLE
THE
DEVON BELLE
34017

The Southern Railway introduced its all-Pullman service to the West Country on 20 June 1947, with Plymouth and Ilfracombe portions making up the formation which normally consisted of twelve cars, although fourteen were needed on busy days. At first these trains ran on Fridays, Saturdays, Sundays and Mondays only, though over the years these days were varied slightly on occasions. The up North Devon portion left Ilfracombe at 12 noon and Exmouth Junction shed often supplied the suitably named 'West Country' Pacific *Ilfracombe* for this prestige duty. This engine, in B R green livery and numbered 34017, is seen near Morchard Road with the maximum rake of eight cars on 2 August 1952. The decorative headboard and side wings add to the already glamorous train.
[Rev. Arthur C. Cawston]

tations were provided at Copplestone (2 miles from Coleford Junction) and Morchard Road (3½ miles). The third :ation was built at Lapford (6 miles). The view above shows the 1.10 p.m. Barnstaple Junction to Exmouth Junction oods waiting in the down loop at Lapford behind 'N' Class Mogul No.31821, 5 June 1964. Below: the 2.20 p.m. x-Ilfracombe d.m.u. leaves Lapford at 3.46 p.m. Now the goods can proceed on its way. As up trains cannot be gnalled out of the down loop the freight will set back down the line in order to collect the tablet from the box before assing through the station once more, this time on the up line. [J. R. Besley]

Having set back, No.31821 is ready to restart the freight on its up journey. The box at Lapford, which also controlled the entrance to a small five-siding yard, was closed on 21 June 1970, since which date two ground frames have sufficed. The down loop is now a siding. [J. R. Besley]

Lapford station, looking towards Coleford Junction, 5 June 1964. The cattle dock and small goods shed are visible on the right, while the down island platform may be seen through the three-arch bridge. The platelayers are going about their daily tasks in the manner which had been traditional on our railways for well over a century. Today much of this work is mechanised, yet the tracks still require the regular attention which is necessary to keep them in perfect order. [J. R. Besley]

A fine action study of the up 'Belle' near Lapford, shortly after its inception in 1947. The immaculate malachite green 'West Country' is No.21C101 *Exeter,* another regular performer on this route during the late 1940s and early 1950s. Originally the whole line was single, but in Southern days only the Coppleston-Umberleigh section remained in this condition. In 1971 the whole route reverted to its former single state. [Rev. Arthur C. Cawston]

THE
DEVON BELLE

A pair of Ivatt Class '2's, Nos.41291 and 41206, wait for the road at Eggesford (9¾ miles from Coleford Junction) whilst on their way back to Exeter after working the 'Exmoor Ranger' special on 27 March 1965. These 2-6-2 tanks, originating on the L M S in 1947, proved highly successful and popular replacements for the Drummond 'M7' 0-4-4Ts in the Barnstaple area. [W. L. Underhay]

A spacious goods yard of five sidings existed at the north end of Eggesford station until April 1965. Above: the 'West Country' Pacific No.34083 *605 Squadron* has set back the 3.25 p.m. Barnstaple to Feltham goods into the long Fox and Hounds siding, which leads to the goods shed and cattle dock, in order to clear the main line for passenger traffic, 5 June 1964. Four miles beyond Eggesford lies King's Nympton followed by Portsmouth Arms, 16¾ miles from Coleford Junction. Below: No.34107 *Blandford Forum* restarts the 4.21 p.m. Exeter (Central) to Barnstaple Junction away from Portsmouth Arms on 4 June 1964. The 'broad gauge' spacing of the passing loop is noticeable, this being inherited from pre-L S W R days. [J. R. Besley]

A down train, hauled by 'Battle of Britain' 4-6-2 No.34063 *229 Squadron,* passes the wooden signal box at Portsmouth Arms. This box was closed on 3 April 1966 and the up loop taken out of use.

The fireman of No.34020 *Seaton* gives up the single line tablet at Umberleigh as the 11.15 a.m. ex-Waterloo swings into the platform with a GUV, three carriages and a Siphon G behind the tender on 9 June 1963. The attractive platform signal box was closed in May 1971. [J. R. Besley]

A typical Taw Valley overhead bridge carries the South Molton road over the tracks at the north end of Umberleigh (4 miles on from Portsmouth Arms). The approaching train is the 8.55 a.m. Ilfracombe to Salisbury stopper, hauled by No.34066 *Spitfire*. Five sidings catered for the local goods traffic, but these were removed after 1965, while the main line was singled in 1971. Four miles beyond Umberleigh lies Chapelton, now an unstaffed halt. [J. R. Besley]

34020

60

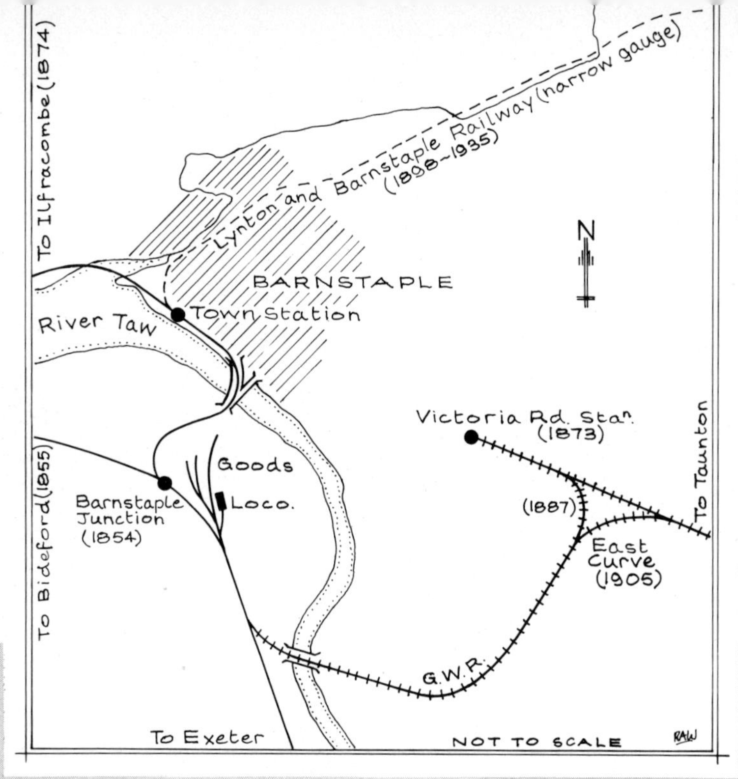

Barnstaple had become the centre of an important network by the later years of the nineteenth century. After the opening of the North Devon line in 1854, the routes to Bideford (1855) and Ilfracombe (1874) were constructed, while the G W R reached Barnstaple's Victoria Road station from Taunton in November 1873. The latter station was connected to Barnstaple Junction by a spur opened in 1887 and the east curve was brought into commission in 1905, allowing through summer trains to bypass Victoria Road and proceed directly to Barnstaple Junction and on to Ilfracombe. The Western route closed for all traffic on 3 October 1966.

'Battle of Britain' Pacific No.34081 *92 Squadron* pulls across to the Ilfracombe line at Barnstaple Junction in September 1959. The lines leading to the right behind the engine are those to Bideford, Torrington and Halwill; the layout was simplified in 1971 following the closure of the Ilfracombe line in 1970. [Derek Cross]

The 5.15 p.m. to Ilfracombe pulls out of Barnstaple Junction (27½ miles from Coleford Junction) behind 'N' Class Mogul No.31853 on 9 July 1964. These Maunsell 2-6-0s were the backbone of the motive power on the North Devon line for almost forty years after their construction in Woolwich Arsenal in 1925, Exmouth Junction shed having 24 on roll as late as 1963. [D. T. Cobbe]

The North Devon Railway established a locomotive depot at Barnstaple Junction in the 1860s, and the wooden structure remained in service until the final years of steam operation a hundred years later. The two roads ran through the shed, the right-hand line to a hoist which was used for repairs to the locomotives when axleboxes, etc., required attention. The adjoining buildings house the offices, repair shops and stores, while the lines to the left are the main goods yard sidings. The Great Western Railway closed its small shed at Victoria Road in 1920, after which its engines were serviced in the Southern loco. Churchward Moguls, based at Taunton shed, were the principal motive power on the Western line trains. At Nationalisation Barnstaple's allocation consisted of eight 'M7' 0-4-4Ts and six 'E1R' 0-6-2Ts, the later 1963 list showing ten of the Ivatt Class '2' 2-6-2 tanks. [H. C. Casserley]

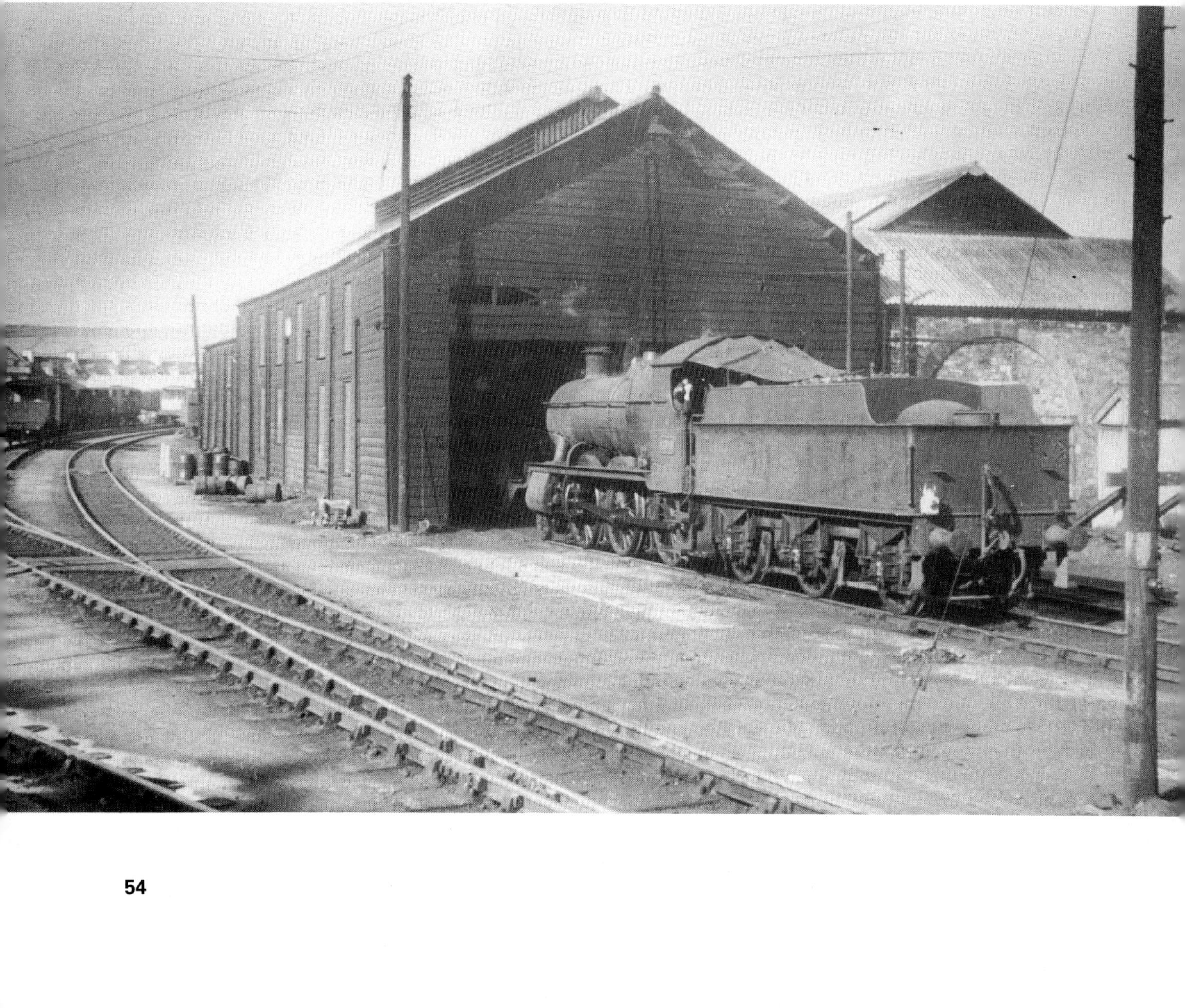

Visiting Exmouth Junction Standard Class '4' 2-6-4 tank No.80039 stands on the fifty-foot turntable in the shed yard at Barnstaple Junction on 12 September 1965. This manually-operated table was large enough to accommodate Moguls but not the larger Bulleid Pacifics which were regular visitors to the depot. The allocation was withdrawn from Barnstaple at the end of 1964 and the wooden shed, which had almost fallen down of its own accord, was finally demolished. [A. R. Butcher]

56 The 'Devon Belle' Pullmans look splendid in the evening sunlight as the heavy train eases over the Taw Bridge. Th rear vehicle is one of the two observation cars which were provided for these trains. Originally an ambulance car these 1918 vehicles were rebuilt as Pullmans in 1921 and modernised as observation cars in 1947, remaining i service on the 'Belle' until it ceased running in 1955. [P. W. B. Semmens

The North Devon line rises to a summit near Copplestone, then drops steadily down to almost sea level at Barnstaple. 'Woolworth' No.31849 steams away on the level out of Barnstaple Junction towards the Taw Bridge and Barnstaple (Town) station on the Ilfracombe line, with a local goods. Unfortunately the freight service to Ilfracombe had only two more months of operation ahead when this photo was taken on 1 June 1964. [J. R. Besley]

A southbound Mogul-hauled freight eases across the Taw Bridge at the prescribed 15 m.p.h. on 24 August 1962. The bridge became redundant when the Ilfracombe line closed on 5 October 1970 and was demolished in recent years. The rounded arches of the road bridge, which was being modernised, may be seen through the cast-iron supports of the railway bridge.
[Pamlin Prints]

A reminder of yesteryear: a narrow gauge (1′ 11½″) train hauled by 2-6-2T No.188 *Lew* and sister engine leaves Barnstaple (Town) station for Lynton in the late 1920s. The Town station, situated on the north side of the Taw estuary, three-quarters of a mile from the junction, was the exchange for the Lynton & Barnstaple trains which, unfortunately, were withdrawn from service on 29 September 1935. [Chapman & Son]

After several miles of easy running the Ilfracombe line suddenly turned nasty beyond Braunton. For six miles down trains had to tackle the climb to Mortehoe summit, the final 3½ miles being a gruelling 1 in 40. Then came a headlong descent down the three-mile gradient to Ilfracombe, two miles of which were at 1 in 36. Western Mogul No.7337 breasts the summit with a Cardiff-bound express on 25 August 1962. [Pamlin Prints]

Four-and-a-quarter miles beyond the Town station lay the station of Wrafton, after which came Braunton, a mile farther north. No.34066 *Spitfire* calls at this latter station with the up 'Atlantic Coast Express' on 20 August 1962. [Pamlin Prints]

'M7' No.30253 and Pacific No.34060 *25 Squadron* at work on Mortehoe bank on 6 June 1960. If the total weight of a passenger train did not exceed 280 tons an assistant engine could be coupled to the front of the train, but a train over that figure had to be banked. No passenger train was allowed to exceed a total of 44 axles. Freight train loading for 'N' Moguls was 'equal 25' while 'M7's were allowed 'equal 11' wagons. [G. P. Brown]

The 3.14 p.m. goods to Barnstaple eases out of the yard at Ilfracombe behind No.31812 on 2 June 1964. Four sidings were available for the goods traffic at this Southern outpost. [J. R. Besley]

A general view of the extensive layout at Ilfracombe on 21 August 1962. The freight traffic was never very heavy and the small goods shed easily sufficed, but eight lengthy carriage sidings were required to store the considerable number of passenger vehicles which were in use on the summer Saturday trains which frequented the line in its prosperous years. [Pamlin Prints]

A party of Scouts entrains at the platform on 16 August 1958. The station at Ilfracombe opened for traffic on 4 July 1874 and the final diesel multiple units were signalled away on 5 October 1970. [A. E. Bennett]

This single-road through shed replaced the original structure in 1929 when the station area was modernised to cope with the increasing traffic. This view of Maunsell Mogul No.1829 must have been taken soon after the opening of the new shed as the engine has not yet been fitted with the smoke deflectors which the class acquired in the early 1930s. No engines were permanently allocated but several were stabled overnight. The 65-foot turntable seen here was replaced by a 70-foot vacuum-operated table in 1947 to allow for the easier turning of the light Pacifics which were introduced at that time. [Aubrey Parminter]

After the line to Barnstaple was opened on 1 July 1854, the passenger service was extended to Bideford on the newly-opened track on 2 November 1855. Stations were provided at Fremington (2¾ miles from Barnstaple Junction) and Instow (6½ miles), Bideford being a further 2¾ miles. Passenger trains reached Torrington on 24 July 1872, then there was a lull in railway construction until 1925 when the North Devon and Cornwall Junction Light Railway was opened from Torrington to Halwill. Standard Class '4' 2-6-4T No.80043 was one of the last steam engines to appear on the line, being seen at the head of the 'Exeter Flyer' excursion at Instow on 12 September 1965. [A. R. Butcher]

Ivatt No.41295 sets out from Torrington with the 12.10 p.m. Halwill goods on 8 July 1961. Torrington itself generated a considerable amount of milk traffic, while clay and cattle were carried on the Halwill extension. A small sub-shed was maintained at Torrington until 1959, stabling three engines sent out from Barnstaple. The single-road building was situated just to the left of the picture. [J. R. Besley]

Torrington station still sported its pre-Nationalisation nameboard as late as 8 April 1961. [J. R. Besley]

No.80043 couples up to the 'Exeter Flyer' at Torrington on 12 September 1965. The line to Halwill closed completely on 1 March 1965, while passenger services were withdrawn between Torrington and Barnstaple, ceasing operation on 4 October of the same year. Milk was conveyed from Torrington until 1973, leaving Bideford as the railhead for the sparse goods traffic still conveyed by rail.
[A. R. Butcher]

THE CHALLENGE TO STEAM

Between the wars the Southern management had directed a considerable amount of capital towards the development of its electric services out of the capital. Much of the suburban traffic and some main line routes on the Central Section were operated by electric multiple units, but consideration was being given to the development of electric locomotives which would be capable of hauling heavy passenger and freight trains over the electrified routes. Chief Mechanical Engineer Bulleid worked with Chief Electrical Engineer Raworth and the result was the 99-ton, 56′ 9″ long, No.CC1 which was built at Ashford Works in 1941.

[W. B. Bushell Collection]

It was hoped that the big new electrics would be capable of operating on heavy wartime freights over the electrified routes and No.CC1 was tested, with considerable success, on 1000-ton goods trains. This view was taken in darkest wartime, 1941, and was originally captioned as 'somewhere in the South of England'. The English Electric equipment on the locomotive contained a booster unit in which current was supplied through a motor to a generator between which was mounted a heavy flywheel which stored kinetic energy by means of which the locomotive could pass over breaks in the conductor rail. A pantograph was also fitted for use in marshalling sidings which possessed overhead wires. [W. B. Bushell Collection]

Again at an undisclosed location, No.CC1 is on test, this time with a heavy passenger train. On such traffic the new machine was tested up to 75 m.p.h. with 750 tons, a very creditable performance. When peace came the engine, with sister No.CC2 and a cousin No.20003, was often to be seen on the smartly timed Newhaven boat trains. The livery, complete with yellow stripes, was typically Bulleid and matched the contemporary 'Merchant Navy' Pacifics.
[W. B. Bushell Collection]

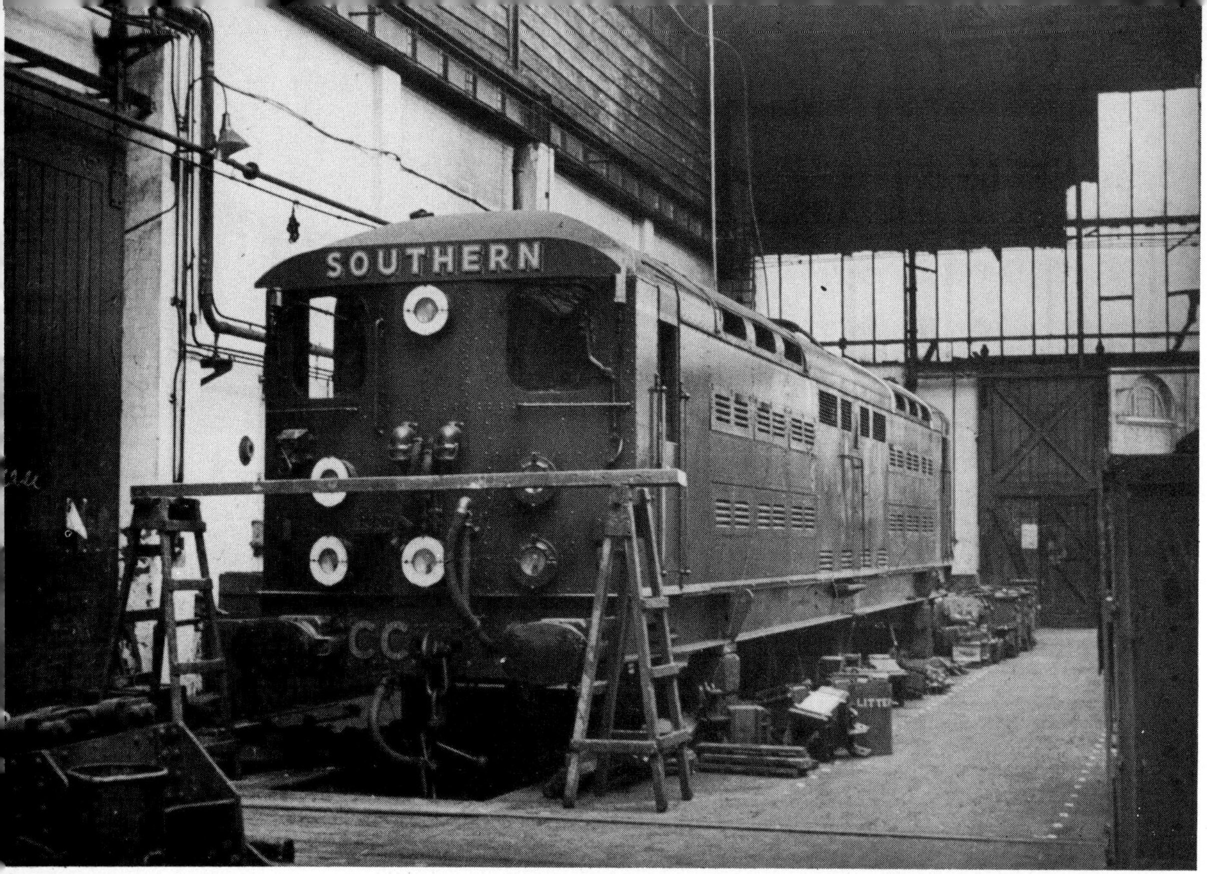

The almost identical No.CC2 under repair at Brighton Works, 28 June 1947. The engines were mounted on two six-wheeled bogies, these having 3′ 6″ wheels of the BFB type. Each axle was powered by a 245h.p. motor. It will be noticed that the disc brackets have been replaced by combined headlamp/discs fitted on each end of the locomotive.
[H. C. Casserley]

No.CC1 was renumbered 20001 by British Railways and was given the ‘non-steam’ livery of black and silver. The scene is Brighton Works on 10 June 1950. These locomotives were equipped with Westinghouse air brakes but also carried an exhauster for operating the vacuum brakes of passenger coaches. They remained in service until 1968 when they were withdrawn from Stewarts Lane depot.
[H. C. Casserley]

The Southern directors decided that an experiment with diesel electric traction should be undertaken and three locomotives were authorised at the end of 1946. Unfortunately the first machine, No.10201, was not complete until early 1951. Here is the second example, No.10202, under construction in Ashford Works on 14 March 1951. The components already in position on the chassis are, from the left, the radiator, fuel tank, 16SVT pressure-charged 16-cylinder 1600b.h.p. diesel engine, electric generator and water tank. The power equipment was supplied by English Electric to the requirements of the Chief Electrical Engineer C. M. Cock, while the design of the mechanical parts of the locomotive was the responsibility of O. V. S. Bulleid. [L. Elsey]

The shapely 135-ton No.10202 tests her stamina on that famous stamping ground, Honiton bank, as she heads the 1.00 p.m. from Waterloo up the 1 in 80 on 28 September 1951. This engine put in many regular appearances on an intensive roster between Waterloo and Exeter. Leaving Waterloo at 1.25 a.m., she returned with the 7.30 a.m. fast from Exeter, then down again on 'The One o'Clock' and finally returned to London on the 5.53 p.m. from Exeter. This involved men from Nine Elms, Salisbury and Exmouth Junction sheds and these senior crews performed well, especially as they were only able to have infrequent runs on the new machine. Also they did not have the comprehensive retraining which was given some years later when diesels became the main motive power. The 1600b.h.p. of these diesels did not match the full power available with a 'Merchant Navy' but the crews appreciated the ease with which the power could be obtained by moving the main controller across to notch five. The firemen were usually disappointed when they found that the big new locomotives were not on the roster as expected and a coal-hungry Bulleid was booked instead! [Brian A. Butt]

The bogies of the new diesel electrics were similar to those of the 'CC' electrics, with the addition of a carrying axle at the outer end. The carrying wheels were 3′ 1″, with 3′ 7″ diameter driving wheels powered by nose-suspended motors on each of the three driving axles of the bogie, giving a 1-Co-Co-1 arrangement for the locomotive. The bogie is outside Ashford Works on 25 June 1951. [L. Elsey]

No.10202 is lowered on to her bogies inside Ashford erecting shop on 25 June 1951. The body shell followed the contours of the Southern's Bulleid post-War stock, being made up from steel panels riveted on to a framework of rolled steel sections. The six hinged covers over the engine compartment were of aluminium. [L. Elsey]

No.10202 at speed near Milborne Port with a down West of England express on 23 August 1952. On the completion of No.10203, the three locomotives were transferred to London Midland Region, where they worked with the ex-L M S. Nos.10000/1 and provided valuable experience in the operation of express diesels prior to the mass production of such units. The three Southern machines were withdrawn in 1964.
[R. E. Toop]

The Southern had been operating diesel electric motive power since 1938. Maunsell had ordered three 350h.p. 0-6-0 shunters from English Electric in 1938. No.2, like her sisters, weighed 55 tons and exerted a tractive force of 30,000lbs.
[K. J. Marden Collection]

A rare 'bird of passage' on Southern metals: Bo-Bo diesel electric No.10800 near Lewes with a Victoria to Brighton semi-fast on 16 July 1952. This 827h.p. hood-type machine was built by the North British Locomotive Company (Glasgow) in 1950 with power equipment by British Thompson Houston Ltd of Rugby. After a year's undistinguished service on L M R the engine was transferred to S R where it was tried out on Central Section passenger services. She soon reverted to goods work before disappearing off the Region. The engine used was a Davey Paxman 16-cylinder RPHXL and the transmission was through four BTH nose-suspended motors, the machine having a total weight just short of 70 tons. [L. Elsey]

XP
TEST UNIT FOR
DIESEL-ELECTRIC
SHUNTING
LOCOMOTIVES.
C.M. & E.E.
DEPT
D.S.3202
BRAKE ON

A 600h.p. diesel engine has been removed from a d.e.m.u. inside Eastleigh diesel depot ready to be transported onto the adjacent works for overhaul, 10 May 1958. [L. Elsey]

A small fleet of 26 diesel-electric 0-6-0 shunters was built for Southern Region in Ashford Works during 1949. Using the well-tried English Electric 350h.p. 6-cylinder engine, these locomotives were basically similar to the L M S standard shunter, but this version had 4′ 6″ driving wheels to match those fitted to the Southern's three existing engines. No.15228 is seen in Ashford Works on 10 March 1951. [L. Elsey]

An S R load car, built on an L B S C R tender underframe with its centre wheels removed. This was used for testing the diesel engines of shunters and d.e.m.u.s and was known to be still in use as recently as 1978. The second vehicle is a wagon used for transporting d.e.m.u. engines to Eastleigh Works for overhaul. The setting is Hastings diesel depot, 26 June 1957. [L. Elsey]

SOME 'TERRIERS' — THEN AND NOW

Confronted by the need for the speedy introduction of efficient new motive power for suburban services in South East London, the newly-appointed Locomotive Engineer of the L B S C R, William Stroudley, designed his 'A1' 0-6-0 tanks and fifty were built in the years 1872-1880. Today, nine of these splendid little engines are still in existence, several in running order, and as a tribute to these centenarians some examples of the class are shown in their working days and in their more recent preserved state.

The first member of the class to enter service was L B S C R No.72 *Fenchurch* in September 1872. After running over half a million miles for the 'Brighton', *Fenchurch* was sold out of service but returned to main line railway stock after Grouping, receiving the Southern Railway number B636. As No.32636 in the B R locomotive list, the 1872 veteran was the oldest locomotive on Southern Region, and is seen here at Newhaven shed along with sister No.32640 and the last engine to be built at Brighton Works, No.80154, on the afternoon of 13 April 1958. [A. R. Butcher]

Fenchurch was sold to the Newhaven Harbour Company in 1898 and worked around the South Coast port under new ownership until her return to the S R at Grouping. After her withdrawal in 1963 she was purchased by the Bluebell Railway in the Spring of the following year and was repainted in black livery, lettered as shown on the right hand side, but named *Fenchurch* on the lefthand side tank. Here the 'Terrier' is seen with restored Wainwright 'P' Class 0-6-0T *Bluebell* near Horsted Keynes on 5 August 1967.

[A. R. Butcher]

Fenchurch steps out before the admiring crowds at the great Locomotive Cavalcade at Shildon on the occasion of the 150th anniversary of the opening of the Stockton & Darlington Railway on 31 August 1975. The 'Terrier' was one of the oldest and smallest machines on view that day and she aroused some of the greatest interest. [A. R. Butcher]

Weighing 28 tons in their final 'A1X' condition, the 'Terriers' were very small engines, but they were exceptionally strong pullers and the boilers steamed well, hence their nickname. They were also called 'Rooters' by the men who worked them, again in reference to their prowess. As the years went by they were outclassed on the heavy suburban duties but found favour on lighter branch line duties and a number were sold to other railways in Britain. This fine photo again shows No.72 at Shildon. [N. E. Preedy]

One of the most famous of all the 'Terriers' was No.40 *Brighton,* which was built in the Works in 1878 and shipped across to France in order to be shown at the Paris Exhibition. The award of a gold medal was proudly announced on the side tanks of the engine for some years afterwards, as may be seen in this view of the tank at Battersea. Worthy of note are the wooden brake blocks with which the 'Terriers' were equipped in their early years.

[L. T. George Collection]

No.40 was one of four 'Terriers' sold to the Isle of Wight Central Railway at the turn of the century, this engine fetching £600 in January 1902. Her new owners gave her the number 11, while the Southern Railway added the name *Newport* in 1928. After some years of motor-fitted working, the former *Brighton* returned to the mainland and took up her old place in the stock lists as No.32640. The veteran remained in active service until November 1963, but on withdrawal was purchased for exhibition at Butlin's Holiday Camp at Pwllheli. However, on 27 January 1973 the 'Terrier' made another trip across Spithead, this time on the ferry *Camber Queen,* seen here at Broad Street Slipway, Portsmouth.

[John Goss]

1878-1973
Returning to the
ISLE OF WIGHT
on loan from
POINTER
POINTER
POINTER
AFP 750B

The erstwhile *Brighton* cum *Newport* at Haven Street, IOW in September 1975, fully restored to Isle of Wight Central black livery. [Peter Paye]

No.11 (ex-No.40) inside Ryde Works in March 1973. This engine had received a Drummond chimney in place of its previous copper cap, and had been rebuilt to A1X specification in 1918, but much of the original machine remains. [T. P. Cooper]

OP
32646

HAVANT
HAYLING ISLAND
32646

No.46 *Newington* was restored to her original livery and exhibited by Messrs Brickwoods Breweries at the *Hayling Billy* public house on Hayling Island, as seen in this photograph. However, the engine returned to the Isle of Wight on 19 June 1979 by way of the Portsmouth-Fishbourne ferry, and on 9 August was handed over to the Wight Locomotive Society by its former owners, Messrs. Whitbreads. It is being retored to its Southern Railway condition as No.W8 *Freshwater*. [D. T. Cobbe]

No.32646, seen at Eastleigh on 22 April 1960, was built in April 1877 as No.46 *Newington*. Sold to the L S W R in 1903 for £500, the engine as L S W R No.734 operated on the Lyme Regis line until 1913, when it was sold to the Freshwater, Yarmouth & Newport Railway on Wight. Renumbered W2 and later W8, she received the name *Freshwater* in 1928. Returning to the mainland in 1949, the engine became No.32646 and continued in operation until November 1963. [D. T. Cobbe]. Below: No.32646 at Havant, after a trip to Hayling Island, 17 July 1958. [H. C. Casserley]

No.32650, on the outskirts of Havant, approaches Langston with the 11.05 a.m. to Hayling Island on 21 July 1963. This engine was built at Brighton in 1876 as No.50 *Whitechapel*, and was probably the most renumbered 'Terrier' of all, becoming in turn L B S C R No.650, Southern Nos.B650, W9 *Fishbourne*, 515S, B R Nos.DS515, 32650 and finally No.10 *Sutton* of the Kent & East Sussex Railway.
[John Goss]

▷

After withdrawal in November 1963, No.32650 was purchased by the Borough of Sutton and Cheam and loaned to the K E S R Preservation Society and renumbered No.10 *Sutton*. The restored engine is seen moving away from Tenterden for Rolvenden on 20 October 1973, this being the first train to run following the granting of a Light Railway Order earlier.
[Brian Morrison]

No.32670, one of the original 1872 batch of 'Terriers' (No.70 *Poplar*) blows off vigorously at Rolvenden on the K E S R line, 18 October 1959. It was appropriate that this 'Terrier' should have been used for the special working, as she had worked here from 1901 as No.3 *Bodiam* in the small company's stock. Returning to main line ownership as No.32670 after Nationalisation, she remained active until November 1963, having worked at Dover, Sittingbourne, Brighton, Newhaven and Hayling Island in the interim.
[Hugh Ballantyne]

32670
32670
SPL

After withdrawal No.32670 languished in the scrap road at Eastleigh shed for some months. This engine retains her original Stroudley copper-capped chimney, a much more graceful stack than those of Drummond design fitted to some members of the class (15 March 1964).

[A. M. Gilmour]

The former *Poplar* was sold to the Kent & East Sussex Preservation Society in April 1964 and soon returned to its earlier haunts. The new owners restored the locomotive to K E S R green livery and her old identity of No.3 *Bodiam*; the 'Terrier' stands with sister engine No.10 *Sutton* at Rolvenden on 24 October 1971. [D. T. Cobbe]

The late 1920s were years of depression and many locomotives were put into store pending better times ahead. No.B678 was laid up when seen in the paint shop at Preston Park, Brighton, 1 October 1927. Some of these locomotives never saw service again, but fortunately this engine was spared the breakers' torch for, two years later in 1929, she was shipped to the Isle of Wight and worked there as No.W4 *Bembridge* (later No.W14). [H. C. Casserley]

A genuine Victorian period piece: No.78 *Knowle* heads a rake of four-wheeled vintage suburban stock shortly after her construction in 1880. British locomotives were kept in fine condition a century ago and on the Brighton, as on most railways, the engines had regular crews who really looked after their 'own' locomotives. [L. T. George Collection]

Bembridge was in poor mechanical shape when she returned to Eastleigh in 1936. However, it was decided to undertake major repairs and complete with a Drummond chimney and reconditioned boiler, she was returned to mainland service as No.2678. Note that the bunker has also been enlarged. Looking smart in Maunsell green livery, the engine is seen at her new home depot at Fratton on 2 October 1937.
[H. C. Casserley]

After the Second World War No.32678 spent some years on the K E S R line before returning to Fratton in 1958 for the Hayling Island service. The 'Terrier' seems to be dwarfed by her modern stock as she pulls away from North Hayling Halt on 25 August 1962. [A. R. Butcher]

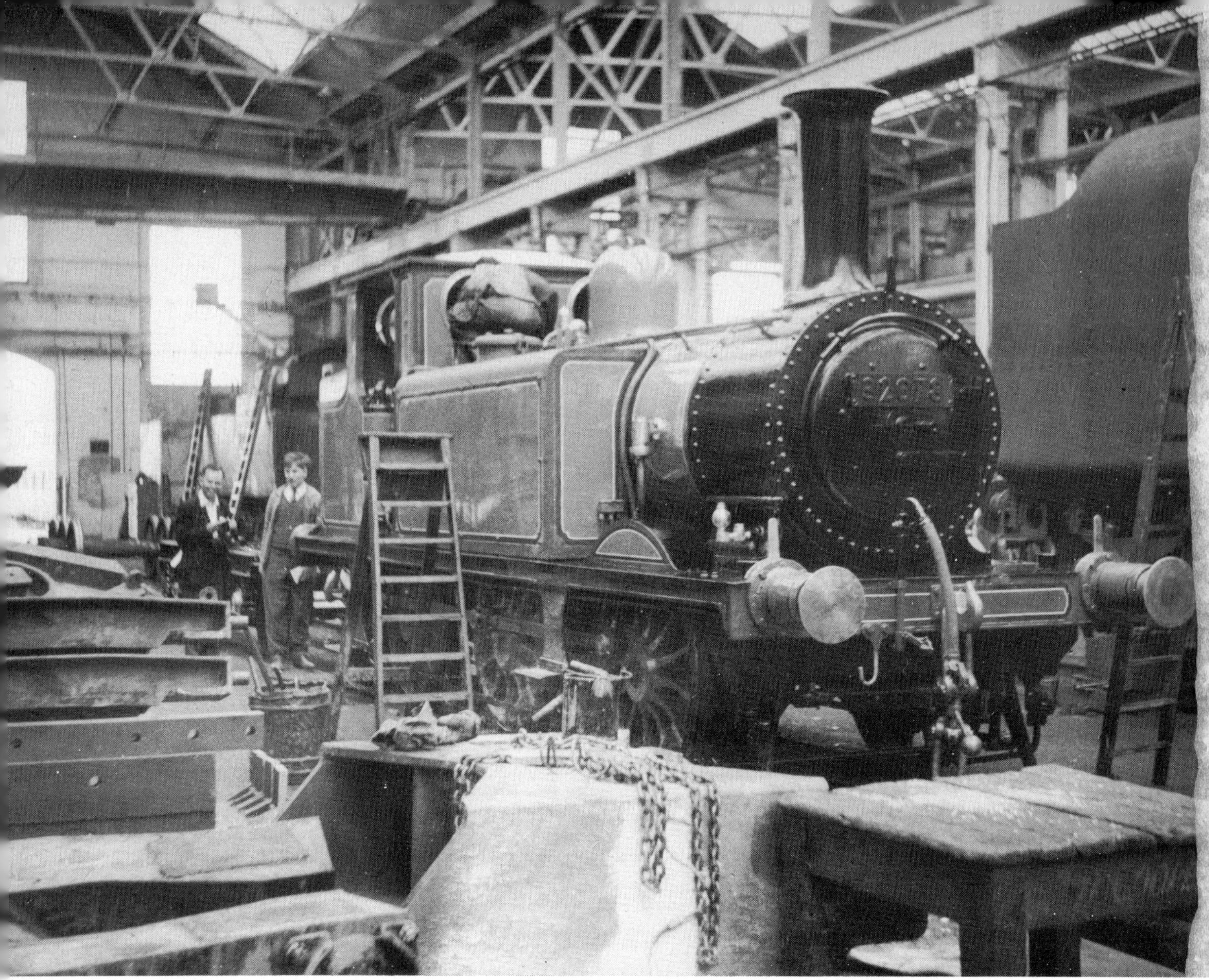

No.32678 worked on Hayling Island until October 1963. She was purchased for restoration in the following year, and is seen in Eastleigh Works on 28 June 1964. There followed many years of static exhibition at Butlin's Minehead Holiday Camp, but now the engine is to be seen on the successfully operating West Somerset Railway. [Maurice Dart]

Postscript: The three other 'Terriers' extant are No.82 *Boxhill* at the National Railway Museum, York, No.55 *Stepney* on the Bluebell Railway and No.62 *Martello* at Bressingham Hall.

MIDLAND
OF THE BORDER
NORTH EASTERN
STEAM
FROM LINES
GREAT WESTERN
STEAM MISCELLANY
BODMIN AND WADEBRIDGE
STANDARD
STEAM
IN ACTION
BRITISH
NARROW GAUG
STEAM
A PICTORIAL SUR
GREAT WESTERN
BRANCH LINE STEAM
DIESELS
ON SCOTTISH REGION
BR
DIESELS
IN THE
LANDSCA
BR
DIESELS
IN ACTION
BRITISH
H. C. CASSERLEY
IRISH RAILWAYS
in the heyday of steam
SOUTHERN
188
THE LYNTON & BARNSTAPLE RAILWAY
OPEAN
EAM
ERN
MOTIVE
THE
WARSHIPS
STEAM
NORTH EASTERN
STEAM
THE
WAINWRIGHT
ASSES
N ACTION
LONDON MIDLAND
STEAM IN ACTION
4
DIESEL - HYDRAULICS
LONDON
RT
BUS
OUTHERN
8F
2-8-0
GREAT
CENTRAL
recalled